T-Shirt Quilts

by Linda Causee

LEISURE ARTS, INC.

Little Rock, Arkansas

Produced by

Production Team

Creative Directors:	Jean Leinhauser
	and Rita Weiss
Photography:	Carol Wilson Mansfield
Book Design:	Linda Causee
Technical Editor:	Ann Harnden

Published by

the art of everyday living
www.leisurearts.com

Library of Congress Control Number: 2013944390
ISBN-13: 978-1-4647-1239-5

Introduction

If your family is like mine, there are a lot of T-shirts in your life. Attend a football game, go to a family reunion, play in the school orchestra, be a member of a team, visit a famous city, be part of a charity event, and the reward is another T-shirt.

What do you do with all the T-shirts you have collected that no one wants to wear anymore? What do you do with your son's T-shirt collection that's taking up valuable space in a dresser drawer long after he's left the house? What about those T-shirts you wore on that long 3-day charity walk. You can't just throw them out. They are full of wonderful messages and great memories.

How about incorporating those messages into delightful quilts that could hang on your walls or keep you warm? That's just what we've done in this book. Instead of using only beautiful fabrics, here you'll find quilt squares made from T-shirts. If you just have a few T-shirts, make a simple wall hanging. If you have a larger collection, you can make a full-size quilt or even a queen-size one.

If you've never made a quilt before, or if you're not sure of your quilting ability, here are the basic instructions you'll need to become a quilter. And, here are the instructions for preparing your T-shirts before you use them in your quilts.

So look in your closets and tear your dresser drawers apart. You're sure to find lots of material to keep your quilting fingers busy for a long time.

I hope you have as much fun as I have had making T-shirt quilts.

Contents

6

10

16

28

32

22

38

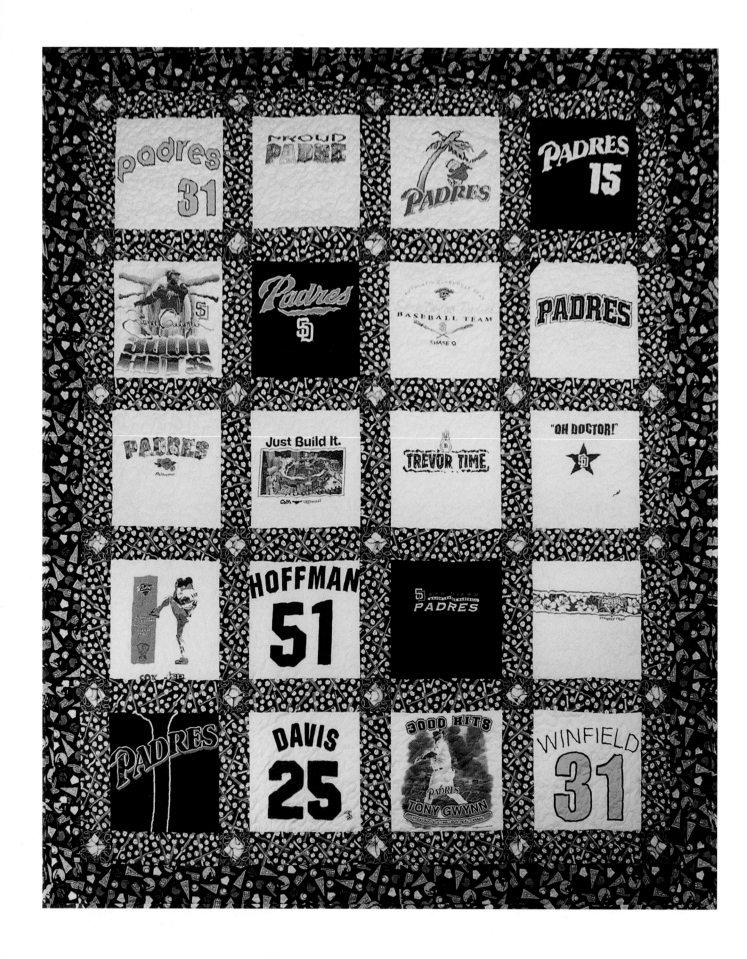

Our Favorite Team

Approximate Size: 92" x 110"

My family's favorite baseball team is the San Diego Padres, and we try to attend as many games as we can. Over the years we have collected many T-shirts either handed out free to all the fans attending or for sale. Instead of just saving those T-shirts in a closet, a T-shirt quilt keeps the memories of great games alive for ages.

Materials

12 assorted T-shirts

$\frac{5}{8}$ yard white baseball fabric (triangles)

$\frac{3}{4}$ yard brown baseball fabric (squares)

$2\frac{1}{4}$ yards bat and ball fabric (sashing)

$2\frac{1}{2}$ yards baseball fabric (border, binding)

$8\frac{1}{2}$ yards lightweight fusible interfacing

queen-size batting

8 yards backing

Optional: *foundation or copy paper*

Cutting

Cornerstone Blocks

Note: *If using Foundation Piecing, you do not need to cut exact pieces to make the cornerstone blocks. If using the Stitch and Flip technique, cut as follows:*

30 squares, 4" x 4", white baseball fabric

120 squares, $2\frac{7}{8}$" x $2\frac{7}{8}$", brown baseball fabric

Sashing

49 strips, $4\frac{1}{2}$" x 15", bat and ball fabric

Border and Binding

8 strips, 7"-wide, baseball fabric (border)

8 strips, $2\frac{1}{2}$"-wide, baseball fabric (binding)

Instructions

1. Choose your T-shirts and prepare, referring to Working with T-Shirts on page 42.

2. Make the Cornerstone Blocks using Foundation Piecing, page 50, or Stitch and Flip, page 48.

3. If using foundation piecing, copy 30 foundations using the pattern on page 9.

4. Cut squares about 3¾" x 3¾" from the white baseball fabric and place on the unmarked side of the foundations centered on space 1; pin in place. **Hint:** *Use a dab of fabric glue stick to hold the fabric in place.*

5. Sew remaining brown baseball fabric pieces to foundation to complete the Cornerstone Square. **Hint:** *Cut 3¼" squares, then cut in half to form triangles to piece to foundation.* **(Diagram 1)** Repeat for remaining squares.

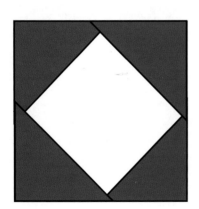

Diagram 1

Finishing

1. Referring to quilt layout on page 9, sew cornerstone and sashing strips together for rows 1, 3, 5, 7, 9 and 11.

2. For remaining rows, sew sashing and T-shirt squares together.

3. Sew rows together.

4. Refer to Finishing Your Quilt, page 59, to complete your quilt.

Stitch and Flip

If using Stitch and Flip, refer to page 48 for instructions and make 30 Cornerstone squares.

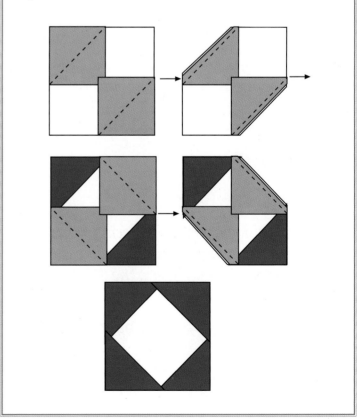

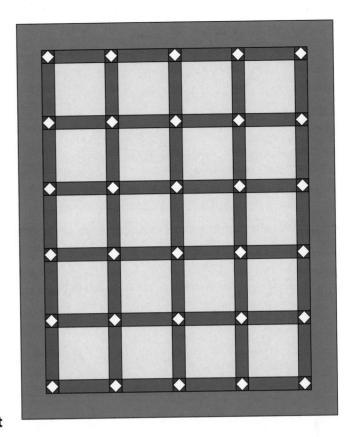

My Favorite Team Quilt Layout

Pattern for Foundation Piecing

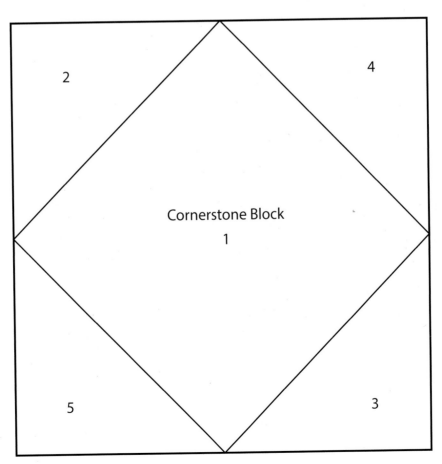

2

4

Cornerstone Block

1

5

3

9

Family Reunions

Approximate Size: 54" x 69"

Every year my friend joins with other members of her extended family for a delightful reunion weekend. Years ago someone decided to add to the fun by supplying T-shirts for everyone. What better way to remember those reunions than a quilt made from the T-shirts family members actually wore.

Materials

5 assorted T-shirts

1 yard burgundy fabric

1½ yards dark blue fabric

1 yard off-white fabric

2¼ yards lightweight fusible interfacing

twin-size batting

3½ yards backing

Optional: *foundation or copy paper*

Cutting

Note: *If using Foundation Piecing, you do not need to cut exact pieces to make the cornerstone blocks. If using Triangles, cut the following:*

Blocks

7 squares, 8¾" x 8¾", burgundy (cut in quarters diagonally)

7 squares, 8¾" x 8¾", off-white (cut in quarters diagonally)

14 squares, 8¼" x 8¼", dark blue (cut in half diagonally)

Finishing

6 strips, 2½"-wide, burgundy (first border)

6 strips, 5½"-wide, dark blue (second border)

6 strips, 2½"-wide, dark blue (binding)

Instructions

T-Shirt Blocks

Choose your T-shirts and prepare, referring to Working with T-Shirts on page 42. Your T-shirts should finish 14½" square after sewing.

Foundation Piecing

1. Referring to Foundation Piecing, page 50, make 28 Triangle Squares using the pattern on page 14. **(Diagram 1)**

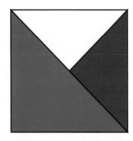

Diagram 1

2. Sew two Triangle Squares together; repeat. **(Diagram 2)**

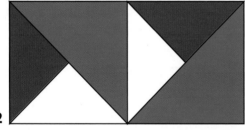

Diagram 2

3. Sew pairs of Triangle Squares together. Make a total of 4 Four Patch blocks. You will have six pairs of blocks leftover to be used for the top and bottom row of your quilt. **(Diagram 3)**

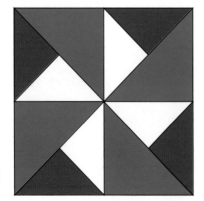

Diagram 3

Finishing

1. Place pairs of blocks, Four Patches and T-shirt squares in rows.

2. Sew blocks in rows, then sew rows together to complete quilt top.

3. Refer to Finishing Your Quilt, page 59, to complete your quilt.

Optional: Sewing with Triangles

If you prefer, you may make the Triangle Squares using triangles rather than using Foundation Piecing.

1. Sew a burgundy and white triangle together. Be sure to have the white triangle on top when sewing all the pairs.

2. Sew the pairs of triangles to the dark blue triangle. Be sure to have the blue triangle on top when sewing.

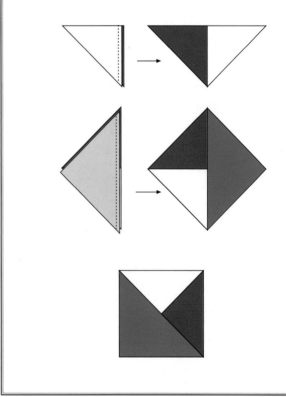

12

Family Reunions Quilt Layout

Pattern for Foundation Piecing

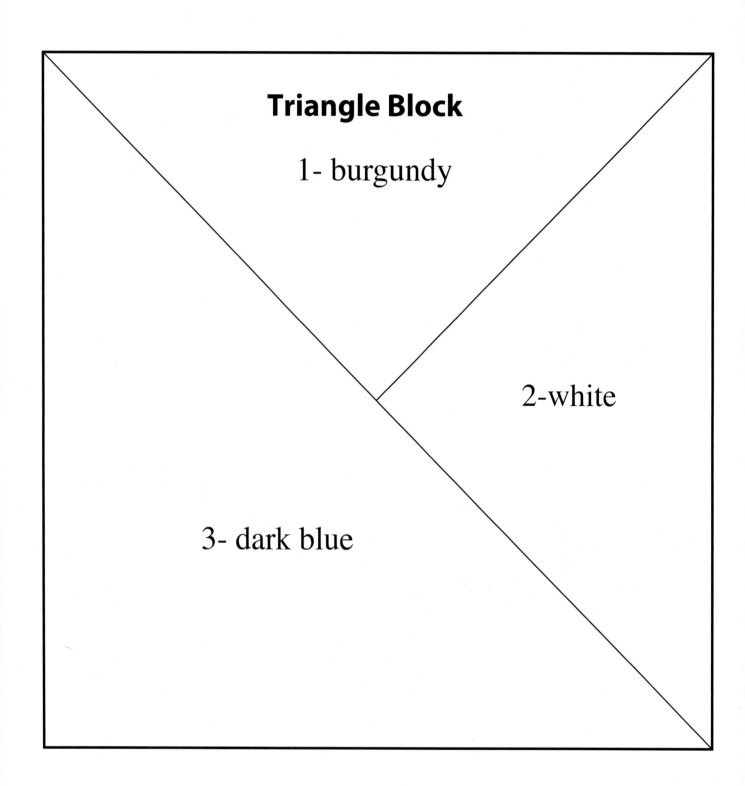

Triangle Block

1- burgundy

2-white

3- dark blue

Bonus: Queen-Size Quilt

Approximate Size: 90 ½" x 105"

If you have at least 13 T-shirts, you can make a queen-size quilt using the layout below.

Materials

13 assorted T-shirts

2 ½ yards burgundy fabric

4 yards dark blue fabric

2 ½ yards off-white fabric

7 yards lightweight fusible interfacing

queen-size batting

6 yards backing

Optional: *foundation or copy paper*

Cutting

Note: *If using Foundation Piecing, you do not need to cut exact pieces to make the cornerstone blocks. If using Triangles, cut the following:*

Blocks

17 squares, 8 ¾" x 8 ¾", burgundy (cut in quarters diagonally)

17 squares, 8 ¾" x 8 ¾", off-white (cut in quarters diagonally)

34 squares, 8 ¼" x 8 ¼", dark blue (cut in half diagonally)

Finishing

8 strips, 2 ½"-wide, burgundy (first border)

8 strips, 5 ½"-wide, dark blue (second border)

8 strips, 2 ½"-wide, dark blue (binding)

Favorite Pastimes

Approximate Size: 82 ½" x 82 ½"

This collection of T-shirts reflects my son's favorite pastimes: sports and good times!

Materials

12 assorted T-shirts

3 yards black print

2 yards dark blue print

2 yards off-white

5½ yards lightweight fusible interfacing

queen-size batting

5 yards backing

Optional: *Foundation or copy paper*

Cutting

Note: *You do not have to cut exact pieces for foundation piecing.*

Finishing

8 strips, 5½"-wide strips, black print
(border)

8 strips, 2½"-wide strips, black print
(binding)

Instructions

1. Choose your T-shirts and prepare, referring to Working with T-Shirts on page 42. Your T-shirts should finish 14 ½" after sewing.

2. Make the Star Blocks using Foundation Piecing, page 50. **(Diagram 1)**

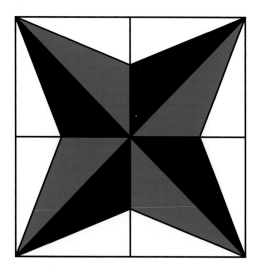

Diagram 1

3. Copy 52 foundations using the pattern on page 20. **(Diagram 2)**

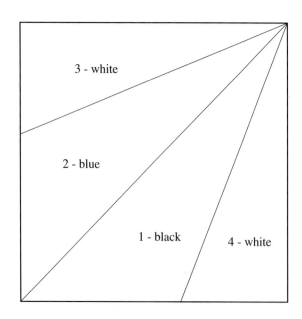

3 - white

2 - blue

1 - black

4 - white

Diagram 2

4. Starting on space 1, pin black fabric to unmarked side of foundation, **Hint:** *Use a dab of fabric glue stick to hold the fabric in place.* **(Diagram 3)**

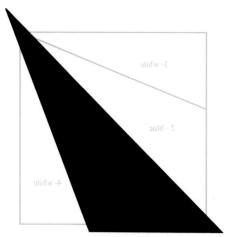

3 - white

2 - blue

4 - white

Diagram 3

5. Continue adding fabric to remaining spaces to cover foundation. Repeat for all 48 foundations. Trim blocks ¼" from outside line. **(Diagram 4)**

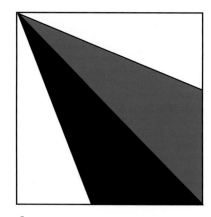

Diagram 4

6. Sew two blocks together in pairs; repeat. **(Diagram 5)**

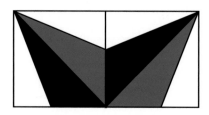

Diagram 5

7. Sew pairs together to complete Star Block. Make 13 Star blocks.**(Diagram 6)**

Finishing

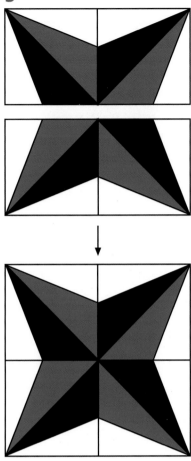

Diagram 6

1. Sew T-shirt and Star blocks together in rows, then sew rows together.

2. Referring to Adding Borders, page 57, sew 5 ½"-wide black print border strips to sides, then top and bottom of quilt top.

3. Refer to Finishing Your Quilt, page 59, to complete your quilt.

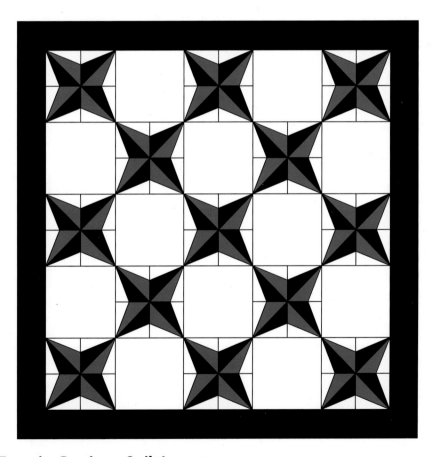

Favorite Pastimes Quilt Layout

Pattern for Foundation Piecing

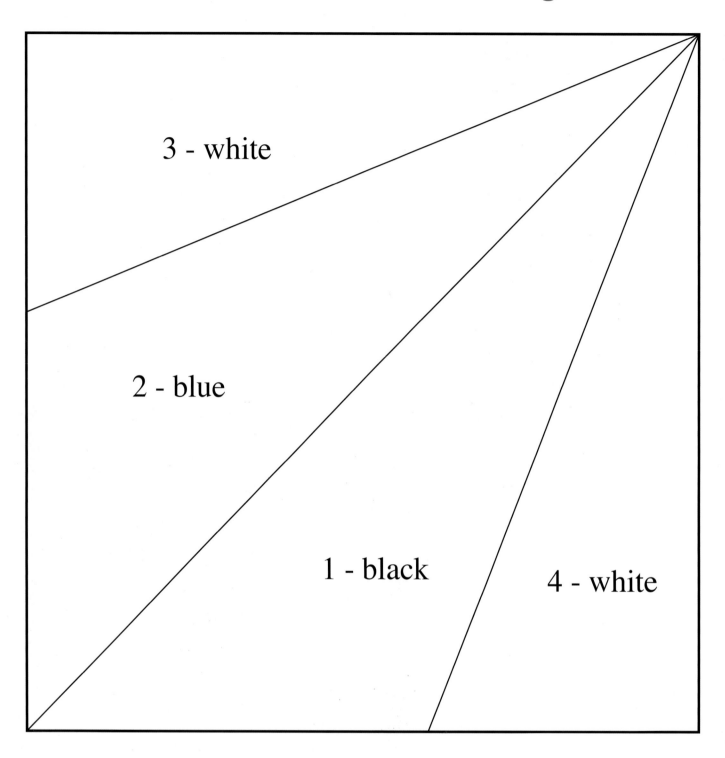

3 - white

2 - blue

1 - black

4 - white

Bonus: Twin-Size Quilt

Approximate Size: 68" x 82 ½"

Fewer pastimes? This twin-size quilt only requires 8 T-shirts.

Materials

8 assorted T-shirts

2 yards black print

1½ yards dark blue print

1½ yards off-white

3½ yards lightweight fusible interfacing

twin-size batting

4 yards backing

Optional: *Foundation or copy paper*

Cutting

Note: *You do not have to cut exact pieces for foundation piecing.*

Finishing

4 rectangles, 7¾" x 15", white

7 strips, 5½"-wide strips, black print (border)

7 strips, 2½"-wide strips, black print (binding)

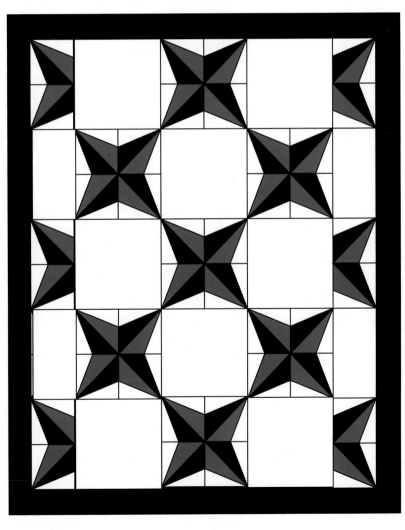

High School Memories

Approximate Size: 80" x 80"

Isaac Bunch had a busy life while he was in school: sports, music, jazz band. When he left for college, he left his mother with T-shirt filled drawers and the instructions that she was not to throw those T-shirts out. His grandmother, however, had other ideas. She asked me to make him a quilt. Now Isaac can "wear" all of his shirts at the same time.

Materials

12 assorted T-shirts

2 yards light green

2 yards medium green

2 yards dark green

8½ yards lightweight fusible interfacing

queen-size batting

5 yards backing

Cutting

Note: *You can sew the blocks with strips and squares or use Strip Piecing. Directions for both techniques are given below. Cut fabric for whichever method you choose.*

Strips and Squares

52 strips, 2½" x 6½", light green

104 squares, 2½" x 2½", medium green

52 strips, 2½" x 6½", medium green

104 squares, 2½" x 2½", dark green

13 squares, 6½" x 6½", dark green

Strip Piecing

9 strips, 2½"-wide, light green

16 strips, 2½"-wide, medium green

7 strips, 2½"-wide, dark green

13 squares, 6½", dark green

Finishing

4 strips, 5½"-wide, dark green (border)

4 strips, 5½"-wide, medium green (border)

8 strips, 2½"-wide, dark green (binding)

Instructions

T-Shirt Blocks

Choose your T-shirts and prepare, referring to Working with T-Shirts on page 42. Your T-shirts should finish 14" square after sewing.

Nine Patch Blocks

1. Make 13 Nine Patch blocks using either Strips and Squares or Strip Piecing below. **(Diagram 1)**

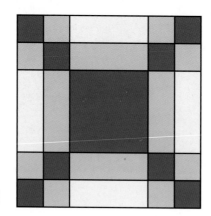

Diagram 1

Strips and Squares

1. Sew dark and medium squares together in pairs; sew pairs together to form a Four Patch. Make 52 Four Patches. **(Diagram 2)**

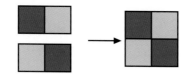

Diagram 2

2. Sew light and medium strips together for a total of 52 pieced strips. **(Diagram 3)**

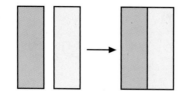

Diagram 3

3. Sew a Four Patch to each end of pieced strips; repeat. **(Diagram 4)**

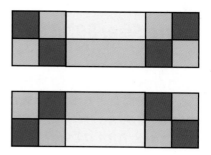

Diagram 4

4. Sew pieced strips to each side of a 6 ½" dark green square. **(Diagram 5)**

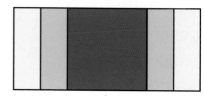

Diagram 5

5. Sew strips from steps 3 and 4 to form a Nine Patch Block. **(Diagram 6)**

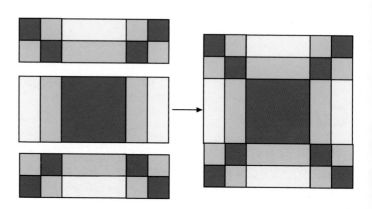

Diagram 6

Strip Piecing

1. Sew dark green and medium green strips together lengthwise. Press seams toward dark green fabric. **(Diagram 7)**

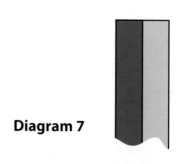

Diagram 7

2. Cut strip set at 2½" intervals. You will need 208 pairs of squares. **(Diagram 8)**

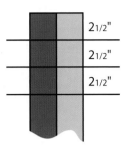

Diagram 8

3. Sew pairs of squares together to form Four Patches. You will need 104 Four Patches. **(Diagram 9)**

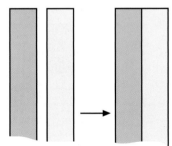

Diagram 9

4. Sew light green and medium green 2½"-wide strips together lengthwise; press seam toward medium green. **(Diagram 10)**

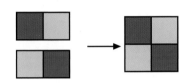

Diagram 10

5. Cut strip sets into 6½" intervals for 52 pieced strips. **(Diagram 11)**

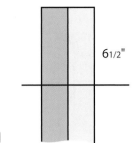

Diagram 11

6. Repeat steps 3, 4, and 5 from Strips and Squares on page 24 to complete blocks. **(Diagram 12)**

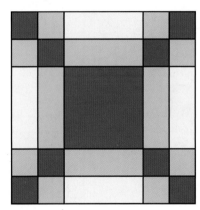

Diagram 12

Finishing

1. Referring to quilt layout on page 26, sew Nine Patch blocks and T-shirt blocks in rows.

2. Sew rows together.

3. Refer to Adding Borders, page 57, to attach border. **Note:** *The photographed quilt has dark green side borders, while the top and bottom borders are medium green.*

4. Refer to Finishing Your Quilt, page 59, to complete your quilt.

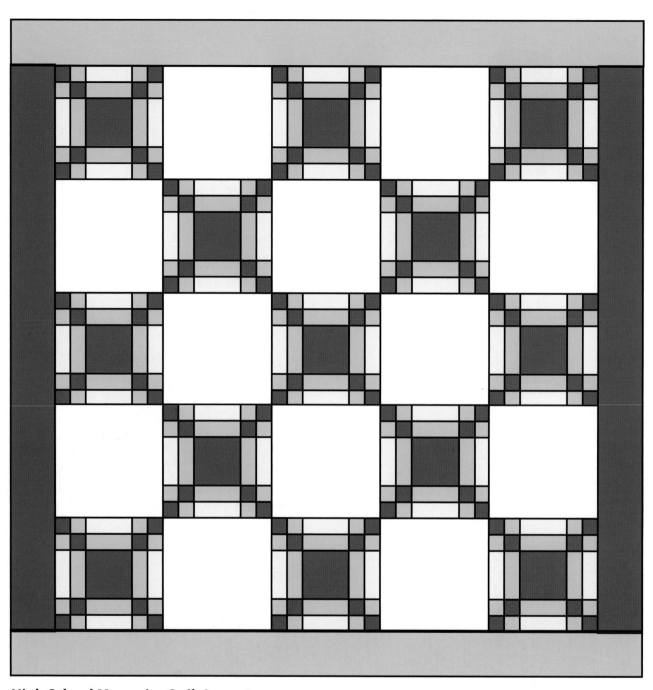

High School Memories Quilt Layout

Bonus: Queen-Size Quilt

Approximate Size: 90" x 108"

More memories; more T-shirts? If you have a few more T-shirts--18 to be exact--you can make a queen-size bed quilt.

Materials

12 assorted T-shirts

2 yards light green

2 yards medium green

2 yards dark green

8½ yards lightweight fusible interfacing

queen-size batting

5 yards backing

Cutting

Note: *You can sew the blocks with strips and squares or use Strip Piecing. Directions for both techniques are given below. Cut fabric for whichever method you choose.*

Strips and Squares

72 strips, 2½" x 6½", light green

144 squares, 2½" x 2½", medium green

72 strips, 2½" x 6½", medium green

144 squares, 2½" x 2½", dark green

18 squares, 6½" x 6½", dark green

Strip Piecing

12 strips, 2½"-wide, light green

21 strips, 2½"-wide, medium green

9 strips, 2½"-wide, dark green

18 squares, 6½", dark green

Finishing

4 strips, 5½"-wide, dark green (border)

4 strips, 5½"-wide, medium green (border)

8 strips, 2½"-wide, dark green (binding)

Our Family

Approximate Size: 70" x 70"

Mom and dad collected T-shirts, and so did their two little boys. Here are some of their favorites. This is the perfect quilt to make when your favorite T-shirts cover many different sizes.

Materials

16 assorted T-shirts

¼ yard orange fabric

¼ yard red fabric

¼ yard green fabric

¼ yard light blue fabric

1½ yards dark blue fabric

fat quarter off-white fabric

3 to 6 yards lightweight fusible interfacing

twin-size batting

3½ to 4 yards backing fabric

Cutting

Blocks

For the scrappy look of this quilt, cut strips from each fabric color in the following widths:

1½"-wide

2"-wide

2½"-wide

3"-wide

Finishing

6 strips, 5½"-wide, dark blue (border)

6 strips, 2½-wide, dark blue (binding)

Instructions

T-Shirt Blocks

Choose your T-shirts and prepare, referring to Working with T-Shirts on page 42.

Note: *The T-shirts used in this quilt are a wide variety of sizes. Use the largest T-shirt design as the size for all the remaining blocks.*

The largest T-shirt design in the photographed quilt is 15" x 15". The remaining T-shirt designs range in size from 6" x 6" to 12" x 12". Therefore the remaining blocks must measure 15" x 15". Sew assorted strips to the smaller blocks until they are each the desired size. This may take one round of strips or two (or more if desired).

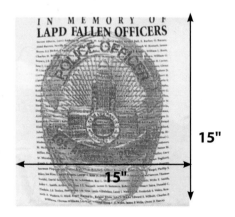

1. Measure one of your T-shirt squares. Choose a strip and cut two strips the size of your T-shirt square. **(Diagram 1)**

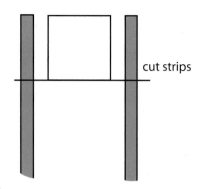

Diagram 1

2. Sew strips to opposite sides of the T-shirt square. Press strips open. **(Diagram 2)**

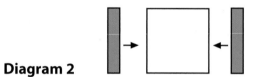

Diagram 2

3. Measure the square including the strips just added; cut two strips to that size. **(Diagram 3)**

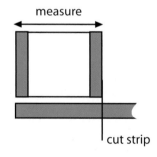

Diagram 3

4. Sew to the top and bottom of the square. **(Diagram 4)**

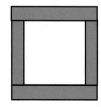

Diagram 4

5. If the block is not the correct size, add another round of strips, repeating steps 2, 3, and 4 above. **(Diagram 5)**

Note: *If your block is larger than needed, trim to size.*

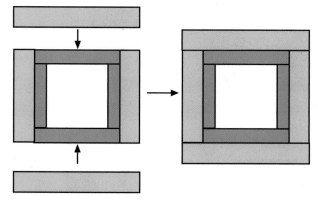

Diagram 5

6. Repeat steps 1 through 5 for remaining T-shirt squares.

Finishing

1. Arrange blocks in four rows of four blocks; sew together in rows, then sew rows together.

2. Refer to Adding Borders, page 57, to add 5½"-wide dark blue border.

3. Refer to Finishing Your Quilt, page 59, to complete your quilt,

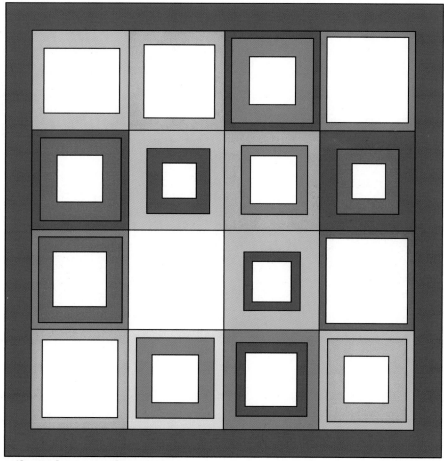

Family T-shirts Quilt Layout

Walk for a Cure

Approximate Size: 48" x 48"

A friend and her daughter participated in the 3-day Susan G. Komen Race for the Cure® to help raise funds for breast cancer research. A quilt made with the T-shirts they wore brings back wonderful memories of that momentous occasion.

Materials

8 assorted T-shirts

fat quarter each of 4 different pink fabrics

⅝ yard pink print fabric (border)

⅜ yard dark pink (binding)

⅝ yard black print

1½ yards lightweight fusible interfacing

twin-size batting

3 yards backing

Cutting

Ribbon Blocks

Notes: *You do not have to cut exact pieces for foundation piecing.*

The ribbon blocks in the photographed quilt are 8" x 8" finished while the T-shirt blocks are 9½" x 9½" finished (10" x 10" cut). Therefore, a 1 ¼" (¾"-wide) border needs to be added so blocks are the same size.

16 strips, 1¼" x 8½", 2 of each pink

16 strips, 1¼" x 10", 2 of each pink

Finishing

5 strips, 4½"-wide, pink print (border)

5 strips, 2½"-wide, dark pink print (binding)

Instructions

T-shirt Blocks

Choose your T-shirts and prepare, referring to Working with T-Shirts on page 42. Your T-shirts should finish 8" or larger.

Ribbon Blocks

1. Referring to Foundation Piecing, page 50, make eight Ribbon blocks—two blocks each of the four pink fabrics. **(Diagram 1)**

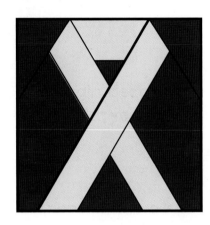

Diagram 1

2. **Note:** *The T-shirt blocks for this quilt are cut 10" square, so strips need to be added to the Ribbon blocks.*

Matching the pink fabric of the ribbon, sew a 1¼" x 8½" strip to opposite sides of a ribbon block; press strips open. **(Diagram 2)**

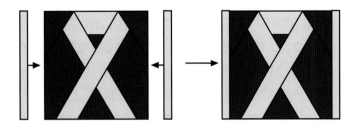

Diagram 2

3. Sew 1 ¼" x 10" pink strips to top and bottom of block. **(Diagram 3)**

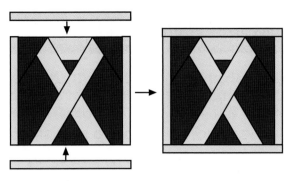

Diagram 3

4. Repeat steps for remaining blocks.

Finishing

1. Arrange blocks alternating Ribbon and T-shirt blocks in four rows of four blocks. Sew blocks in rows, then sew rows together.

2. Refer to Adding Borders, page 57, sew 4½"-wide pink print border strips to sides, then to top and bottom of quilt top.

3. Referring to Finishing Your Quilt, page 59, complete your quilt.

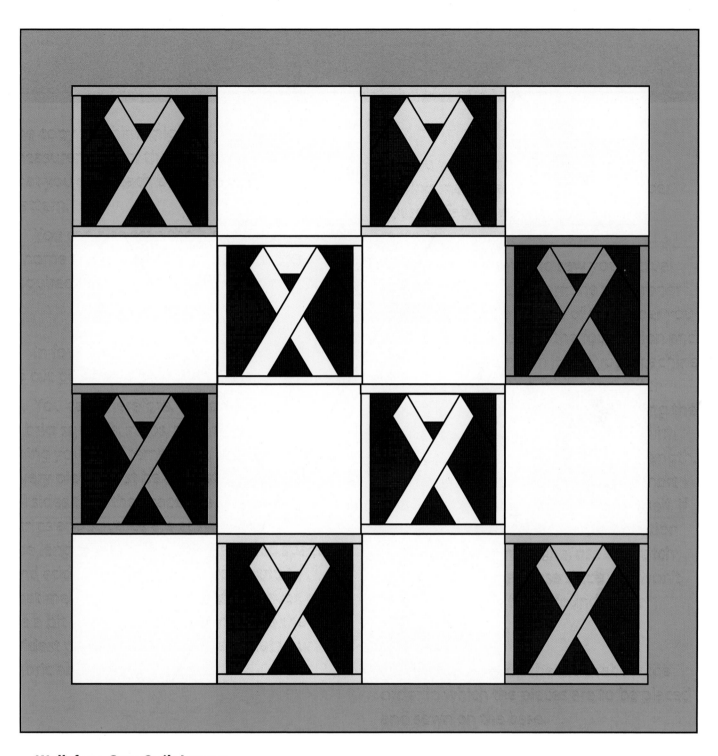

Walk for a Cure Quilt Layout

Pattern for Foundation Pieceing

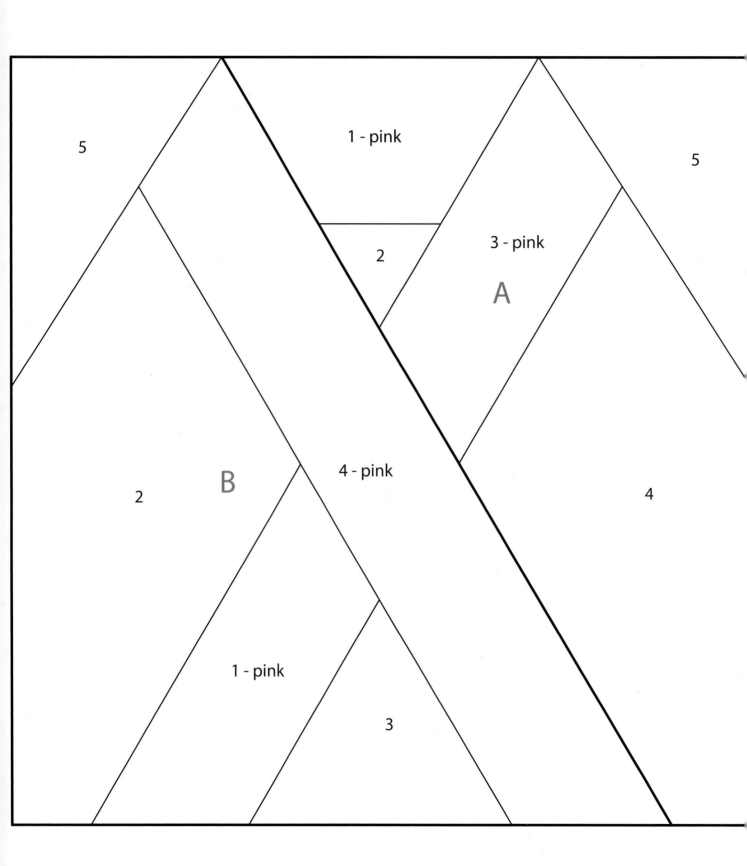

Bonus: Twin-Size Quilt

Approximate Size: 68" x 88"

If you have 17 T-shirts, you can make a quilt for a twin bed.

Materials

17 assorted T-shirts

½ yard each of 4 different pink fabrics

2 ½ yards pink print fabric (border)

¾ yard dark pink (binding)

2 ½ yards black print

3 yards lightweight fusible interfacing

twin-size batting

4 yards backing

Cutting

Ribbon Blocks

Notes: *You do not have to cut exact pieces for foundation piecing.*

The ribbon blocks in the photographed quilt are 8" x 8" finished while the T-shirt blocks are 9½" x 9½" finished (10" x 10" cut). Therefore, a 1¼" (¾"-wide finished) border needs to be added so blocks are the same size.

36 strips, 1¼" x 8½" , 2 of each pink

36 strips, 1¼" x 10" , 2 of each pink

Finishing

7 strips, 4½"-wide, pink print (border)

7 strips, 2½"-wide, dark pink print (binding)

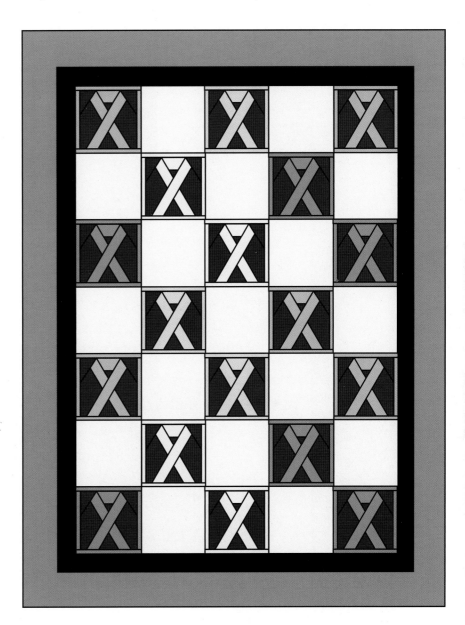

A Few of Dad's Favorites

Approximate Size: 49" x 84"

Here is a quilt made from a collection of T-shirts from some of my father's favorite places and events.

Materials

8 assorted T-shirts

⅝ yard each of cream, tan, light blue and dark blue

1½ yards dark blue (first border, binding)

⅞ yard cream (second border)

3½ yards lightweight fusible interfacing

twin-size batting

3½ yards backing

Cutting

Striped Blocks

Pieced Technique

8 strips, 4" x 14½", each of cream, tan, light blue and dark blue

or

Strip-pieced Technique

4 strips, 4"-wide, each of cream, tan, light blue and dark blue

Finishing

7 strips, 4"-wide, dark blue (first border)

7 strips, 4"-wide, cream (second border)

7 strips, 2½"-wide, dark blue (binding)

Instructions

T-shirt Blocks

Choose your T-shirts and prepare, referring to Working with T-Shirts on page 42.

Striped Blocks

Pieced Technique

1. Sew a cream, light blue, tan and dark blue strip together. **(Diagram 1)**

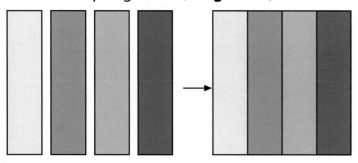

Diagram 1

2. Press seams in one direction.

3. Repeat for a total of seven Striped Blocks.

Strip-Pieced Technique

1. Sew cream, light blue, tan and dark blue 4"-wide strips together; press seams in one direction. **(Diagram 2)**

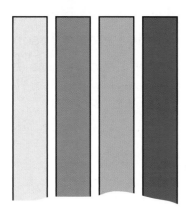

Diagram 2

2. Cut strip set at 14½" intervals to make a Striped Block. Repeat for a total of seven Striped blocks. **(Diagram 3)**

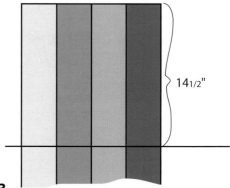

14½"

Diagram 3

Finishing

1. Arrange Striped and T-shirt blocks alternating in five rows of three blocks; sew blocks together in rows, then sew rows together. **(Diagram 4)**

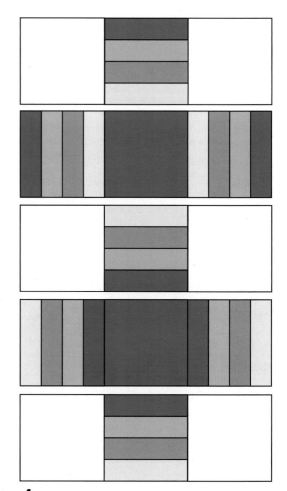

Diagram 4

2. Refer to Mitered Borders, page 58, to sew borders to quilt top. **Note:** *Sew cream and dark blue strips together lengthwise and use as a single border.* **(Diagram 5)**

Diagram 5

3. Refer to Finishing Your Quilt, page 59, to complete your quilt.

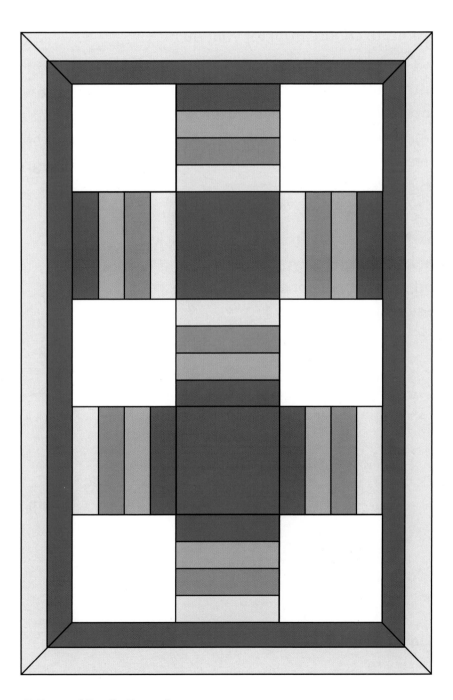

A Few of Dad's Favorites

Working with T-Shirts

The T-shirt blocks for the quilts in this book need to be prepared before using in your quilt. Choose T-shirts with a similar theme. Some T-shirts have a design on the front and back, therefore you have more designs to choose from for your quilt.

The supplies you will need are a rotary cutter, cutting mat, and an acrylic ruler. **Note:** *Although any size ruler can be used, a large square acrylic ruler (at least 15" x 15") is recommended as it will make cutting the design area easier.*

Cut off the sleeves from your T-shirts, then cut away the fronts from the backs. Look at designs on your chosen T-shirts and start with the one with the largest design area. **(Diagram 1)**

Place the T-shirt on your cutting mat and using your acrylic ruler and rotary cutter, cut the design at least ¼" from the edges of the design. **Note:** *Since most of the quilt designs use square blocks, cut the design in a square.*

Use the largest design as the guide for cutting all designs. For example, if the largest design area is 14" x 14", you will need to cut all your T-shirts at least 15" x 15". Try centering the design as much as possible. **(Diagram 2)**

Diagram 2

Diagram 1

Sometimes this will not work due to the fact that designs are usually printed closer to the top of the shirt so some of your designs will not be centered. **(Diagram 3)**

Diagram 3

Once all of your T-shirts are cut, you need to iron fusible lightweight interfacing (cut to the same size) to the wrong side of the squares since T-shirts are made from stretchy knit fabric.

First, press the shirt square on the wrong side. **Note:** *Most T-shirt designs have a "rubberized" finish that will stick to your iron, therefore iron on the wrong side.*

Keeping the T-shirt square wrong side up on the ironing board, center interfacing square (same size as your cut T-shirt squares) over design. Lift iron up and down rather than side to side to avoid wrinkles being formed. Be sure to follow directions for the interfacing you are using for the correct temperature setting for your iron.

Using a rotary cutter and acrylic ruler, trim T-shirt so it measures 14½" x 14½" or size specified in the instructions.

Repeat steps for remaining shirts.

Making a Quilt

Fabric

For over a hundred years, quilts have been made with 100% cotton fabric, the choice for most quilters.

There are many properties in cotton that make it especially well-suited to quilt making. There is less distortion in cotton fabric, thereby affording the quilter greater security in making certain that even the smallest bits of fabric will fit together. Because a quilt block made of cotton can be ironed flat with a steam iron, a puckered area, created by mistake, can be fixed. The sewing machine needle can move through cotton with a great deal of ease when compared to some synthetic fabrics. While you may find that quilt artists today often use other kinds of fabric, to create the quilts quickly and accurately, 100% cotton is strongly recommended.

Cotton fabric today is produced in so many wonderful and exciting combinations of prints and solids that it is often difficult to pick colors for your quilt. We've chosen our favorite colors for these quilts, but don't be afraid to make your own choices.

For years, quilters were advised to prewash all of their fabric to test for colorfastness and shrinkage. Now most quilters don't bother to prewash all of their fabric but they do pretest it. Cut a strip about 2" wide from each piece of fabric that you will use in your quilt. Measure both the length and the width of the strip. Then immerse it in a bowl of very hot water, using a separate bowl for each piece of fabric. Be especially concerned about reds and dark blues because they have a tendency to bleed if the initial dyeing was not done properly. If it's one of your favorite fabrics that's bleeding, you might be able to salvage the fabric. Try washing the fabric in very hot water until you've washed out all of the excess dye. Unfortunately, fabrics that continue to bleed after they have been washed repeatedly will bleed forever. So eliminate them right at the start.

Now, take each one of the strips and iron them dry with a hot iron. Be especially careful not to stretch the strip. When the strips are completely dry, measure and compare them to your original strip. If all of your fabric is shrinking the same amount, you don't have to worry about uneven shrinkage in your quilt. When you wash the final quilt, the puckering that will result may give you the look of an antique quilt. If you don't want this look, you are going to have to wash and dry all of your fabric before you start cutting. Iron the fabric using some spray starch or sizing to give fabric a crisp finish.

If you are never planning to wash your quilt, i.e. your quilt is intended to be a wall hanging such as many of the quilts in this collection, you could eliminate the pre-testing process. You may run the risk, however, of some future relative to whom you have willed your quilts deciding that the wall hanging needs freshening by washing.

Before beginning to work, make sure that your fabric is absolutely square. If it is not, you will have difficulty cutting square pieces. Fabric is woven with crosswise and lengthwise threads. Lengthwise threads should be parallel to the selvage (that's the finished edge along the sides; sometimes the fabric company prints its name along the selvage), and crosswise threads should be perpendicular to the selvage. If fabric is off grain, you can usually straighten it by pulling gently on the true bias in the opposite direction to the off-grain edge. Continue doing this until the crosswise threads are at a right angle to the lengthwise threads.

Rotary Cutting

Supplies for Rotary Cutting

For rotary cutting, you will need three important tools: a rotary cutter, a mat and an acrylic ruler. There are currently on the market many different brands and types. Choose the kinds that you feel will work for you. Ask your quilting friends what their preferences are, then make your decision.

There are several different rotary cutters now available with special features that you might prefer such as the type of handle, whether the cutter can be used for both right- and left-handed quilters, safety features, size, and finally the cost.

Don't attempt to use the rotary cutter without an accompanying protective mat. The mat will not only protect your table from becoming scratched, but it will protect your cutter as well. The mat is self-healing and will not dull the cutting blades. Mats are available in many sizes, but if this is your first attempt at rotary cutting, an 18" x 24" mat is probably your best choice. When you are not using your mat, be sure to store it on a flat surface. Otherwise your mat will bend. If you want to keep your mat from warping, make certain that it is not sitting in direct sunlight; the heat can cause the mat to warp. You will not be able to cut accurately when you use a bent or warped mat.

Another must for cutting accurate strips is a strong straight edge. Acrylic rulers are the perfect choice for this. There are many different brands of acrylic rulers on the market, and they come in several widths and lengths. Either a 6" x 24" or a 6" x 12" ruler will be the most useful. The longer ruler will allow you to fold your fabric only once while the smaller size will require folding the fabric twice. Make sure that your ruler has ⅛" increment markings in both directions plus a 45-degree marking.

Cutting Strips With a Rotary Cutter

Before beginning to work, iron your fabric to remove the wrinkles. Fold the fabric in half, lengthwise, bringing the selvage edges together. Fold in half again. Make sure that there are no wrinkles in the fabric.

Now place the folded fabric on the cutting mat. Place the fabric length on the right side if you are right-handed or on the left side if you are left-handed. The fold of the fabric should line up along one of the grid lines printed on the mat. **(Diagram 1)**

Right-handed

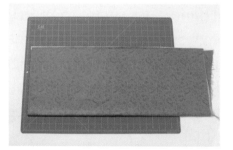

Left-handed

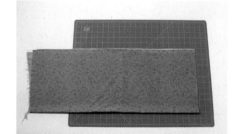

Diagram 1

Straighten one of the cut edges first. Lay the acrylic ruler on the mat near the cut edge; the ruler markings should be even with the grid on the mat. Hold the ruler firmly with your left hand (or, with your right hand if you are left-handed). To provide extra stability, keep your small finger off the mat. Now hold the rotary cutter with blade against the ruler and cut away from you in one quick motion. **(Diagram 2)**

Diagram 2

Carefully turn the fabric (or mat with the fabric) so the straightened edge is on the opposite side. Place the ruler on the required width line along the cut edge of the fabric and cut the strip, making sure that you always cut away from you —

Diagram 3

46

never toward you. Cut the number of strips called for in the directions. **(Diagram 3)**

After you have cut a few strips, you will want to check to make certain that your fabric continues to be perfectly square. To do this, just line up the crosswise markings along the folded edge of fabric and the lengthwise edge of the ruler next to the end of fabric you are cutting. Cut off uneven edge. If you fail to do this, your strips may be bowed with a "v" in the center, causing your piecing to become inaccurate as you continue working.

Cutting Squares and Rectangles

Now that you have cut your strips, you can begin to cut squares or rectangles. Place a stack of strips on the cutting mat. You will be more successful in cutting — at least in the beginning — if you work with no more than four strips at a time. Make certain that the strips are lined up very

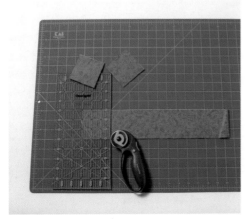

Diagram 4

evenly. Following the instructions given for the quilt, cut the required number of squares or rectangles. **(Diagram 4)**

Cutting Triangles

Once your squares are cut, you can cut triangles, including half-square triangles and triangle squares.

Half-Square Triangles

The short sides of a half-square triangle are on the short grain of the fabric. This is especially necessary if the short edges are on the outer side of the block.

Cut the squares the size indicated in the instructions, then cut the square in half diagonally. **(Diagram 5)**

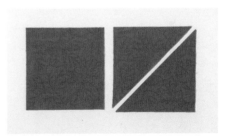

Diagram 5

Triangle Squares

These are squares made up of two different-colored triangles. To make these squares, you can cut individual triangles as described in Half-Square Triangles above. Then sew two triangles together. A quick method, especially if you have several triangle squares with the same fabric, is to sew two squares together. Then draw a diagonal line on the wrong side of the lighter square. Place two squares right sides together and sew ¼" from each side of the drawn line.

Cut along the drawn line, and you have created two triangle squares. **(Diagram 6)**

Stitch and Flip

This is a method for quickly creating triangles and octagons or trapezoids.

Instead of cutting these shapes, you cut and sew squares or rectangles together. **(Diagram 7)**

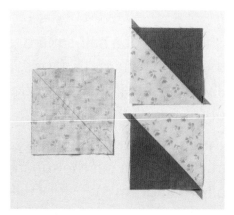

Diagram 6

Diagram 8

Diagram 7

Diagram 9

With right sides together, place a small square in the corner of a larger square or rectangle. You then sew diagonally from corner to corner of the small square. **(Diagram 8)**

Trim the corner about ¼" from the seam line. **(Diagram 9)**

Flip the triangle over and iron. **(Diagram 10)**

Repeat at the other corners. **(Diagram 11)**

Strip Piecing

Strip piecing is a much faster and easier method of making quilts rather than creating the blocks piece by piece. With this method, two or more strips are sewn together and then cut at certain intervals. For instance, if a block is made up of several 3" finished squares, cut 3 ½"-wide strips along the crosswise grain. **(Diagram 12)**

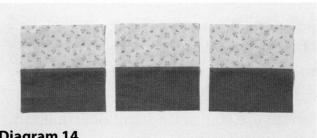

Diagram 12

Diagram 10

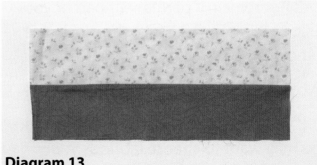

Diagram 13

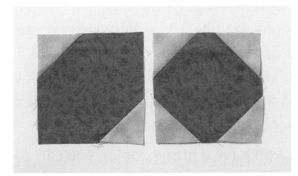

Diagram 11

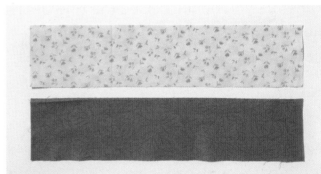

Diagram 14

49

With right sides together, sew two strips along the length. The seam should be pressed to the dark side of the fabric. **(Diagram 13, Page 49)**

Cut across strips at 3 ½" intervals to create pairs of 3 ½" squares. **(Diagram 14, Page 49)**

Foundation Piecing

Materials

Before you begin, decide the kind of foundation on which you are planning to piece the blocks.

Paper

The most popular choice is paper. It's readily available and fairly inexpensive. You can use copy paper, newsprint, tracing paper–even computer paper. The paper does not remain a permanent part of your quilt, as it is removed once the blocks are completely sewn.

Fabric

If you choose to hand piece your block, you may want to choose fabric as your foundation. Just remember that fabric is not removed after you make your block so you will have another layer to quilt through. This may be a problem if you are planning to hand quilt. Using fabric might be an advantage, however, if you want to use some non-traditional quilting fabrics, such as silk or satin, since the fabric foundation will add stability to the block. Fabric makes a good choice for crazy quilts. If you do decide to use fabric, choose a lightweight and light-colored fabric, such as muslin, that will allow you to see through for ease in tracing.

Other Materials

Another option for foundation materials is Tear Away™ or Fun-dation™, translucent non-woven materials combining both the advantages of both paper and fabric. They are easy to see through, but like paper they can be removed with ease.

Currently a new kind of foundation material has appeared in the market place: a foundation paper that dissolves in water after use. Two companies, W.H. Collins and EZ Quilting by Wrights, are producing this product.

Preparing the Foundation

Place your foundation material over your chosen block and trace the block pattern. Use a ruler and a fine-line pencil or permanent marker, and make sure that all lines are straight. Sometimes short dashed lines or even dotted lines are easier to make. Be sure to copy all numbers. You will need to make a foundation for each block you are planning to use.

If you have a home copier, you can copy your tracing on the copy machine. Since the copy machine might slightly alter the measurements of the block, make certain that you copy each block from the original pattern.

You can also scan the block if you have a home scanner and then print out the required number of blocks.

Cutting the Fabric

In foundation piecing, you do not have to cut perfect shapes!

You can, therefore, use odd pieces of fabric: squares, strips, rectangles. The one thing you must remember, however, is that every piece must be at least ¼" larger on all sides than the space it is going to cover. Strips and squares are easy: just measure the length and width of the needed space and add ½" all around. Cut your strip to that measurement. Triangles, however, can be a bit tricky. In that case, measure the widest point of the triangle and cut your fabric about ½" to 1" wider.

Other Supplies for Foundation Piecing

Piecing by hand:

You will need a reasonably thin needle such as a Sharp size 10; a good-quality, neutral-colored thread such as a size 50 cotton; some pins, a glue stick; fabric scissors; muslin or fabric for the bases.

Piecing by machine:

You will need a cleaned and oiled sewing machine; glue stick; pins, paper scissors, fabric scissors, foundation material.

Before beginning to sew your actual block by machine, determine the proper stitch length. Use a piece of the paper you are planning to use for the foundation and draw a straight line on it. Set your machine so that it sews with a fairly short stitch (about 20 stitches per inch). Sew along the line. If you can tear the paper apart with ease, you are sewing with the right length. You don't want to sew with such a short stitch that the paper falls apart by itself. If you are going to use a fabric foundation with the sewing machine, use the stitch length you normally use since you won't be removing the fabric foundation.

Using a Pattern

The numbers on the block show the order in which the pieces are to be placed and sewn on the base.

It is extremely important that you follow the numbers; otherwise the entire process won't work.

Making the Block

The important thing to remember about making a foundation block is that the fabric pieces go on the unmarked side of the foundation while you sew on the printed side. The finished blocks are a mirror image of the original pattern.

Step 1: Hold the foundation up to a light source - even a window pane - with the unmarked side facing. Find the space marked 1 on the unmarked side and put a dab of glue there. Place the fabric right side up on the unmarked side on Space 1, making certain that the fabric overlaps at least ¼" on all sides of space 1. **(Diagram 15)**

Step 2: Fold the foundation along the line between Space 1 and Space 2. Cut the fabric so that it is ¼" from the fold. **(Diagram 16)**

Step 3: With right sides together, place Fabric Piece 2 on Fabric Piece 1, making sure that the edge of Piece 2 is even with the just-trimmed edge of Piece 1. **(Diagram 17)**

Step 4: To make certain that Piece 2 will cover Space 2, fold the fabric piece back along the line between Space 1 and Space 2. **(Diagram 18)**

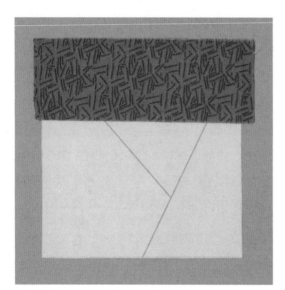

Diagram 15

Diagram 17

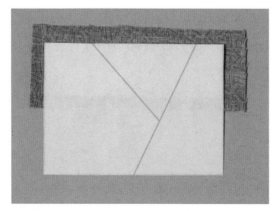

Diagram 16

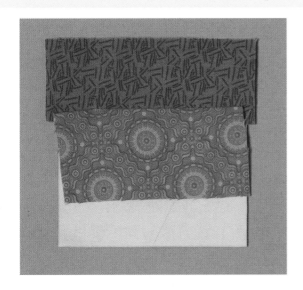

Diagram 18

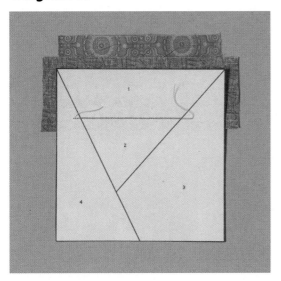

Diagram 19

Step 5: With the marked side of the foundation facing up, place the piece on the sewing machine (or sew by hand), holding both Piece 1 and Piece 2 in place. Sew along the line between Space 1 and Space 2. **(Diagram 19)**

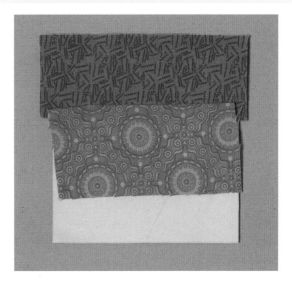

Diagram 20

If you use a small stitch, it will be easier to remove the paper later. Start sewing about two or three stitches before the beginning of the line and end your sewing two or three stitches beyond the line. This will allow the stitching to be held in place by the next round of stitching rather than by backstitching.

Step 6: Turn the work over and open Piece 2. Finger press the seam open. **(Diagram 20)**

Step 7: Turning the work so that the marked side is on top, fold the foundation forward along the line between Space 1+2 and Space 3. Trim about ⅛" to ¼" from the fold. It is easier to trim the paper if you pull the paper away from the stitching. If you use fabric as your foundation, fold the fabric forward as far as it will go and then start to trim. **(Diagram 21, Page 54)**

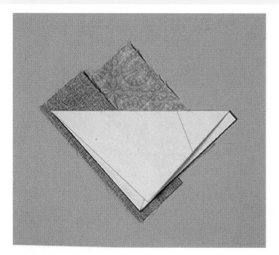

Diagram 21

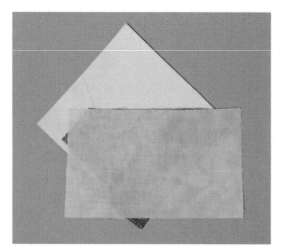

Diagram 22

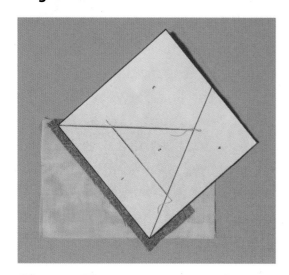

Diagram 23

Step 8: Place Fabric #3 right side down even with the just-trimmed edge. **(Diagram 22)**

Step 9: Turn the block over to the marked side and sew along the line between Space 1+2 and Space 3. **(Diagram 23)**

Step 10: Turn the work over, open Piece 3 and finger press the seam. **(Diagram 24)**

Step 11: In the same way you have added the other pieces, add Piece #4 to

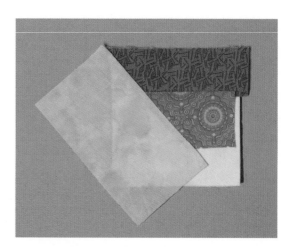

Diagram 24

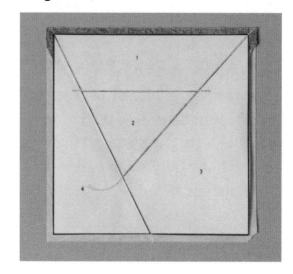

Diagram 25

complete this block. Trim the fabric ¼" from the edge of the foundation. The foundation-pieced block is completed. **(Diagram 25)**

After you have finished sewing a block, don't immediately remove the paper. Since you are often piecing with tiny bits of fabric, grainline is never a factor. Therefore, some of the pieces may have been cut on the bias and may have a tendency to stretch. You can eliminate any problem with distortion by keeping the paper in place until all of the blocks have been sewn together. If, however, you want to remove the paper, stay stitch along the outer edge of the block to help keep the block in shape.

Sewing Multiple Sections

Some blocks in foundation piecing, such as *Favorite Pastimes*, are created with two or more sections. These sections, which are indicated by letters, are individually pieced and then sewn together. The cutting line for these sections is indicated by a bold line. Before you start to make any of these multi-section blocks, begin by cutting the foundation piece apart so that each section is worked independently. Leave a ¼" seam allowance around each section.

Step 1: Following the instructions above for Making the Block, complete each section. Then place the sections right side together. Pin the corners of the top section to the corners of the bottom section. **(Diagram 26)**

Step 2: If you are certain that the pieces are aligned correctly, sew the two sections together using the regular stitch length on the sewing machine. **(Diagram 27)**

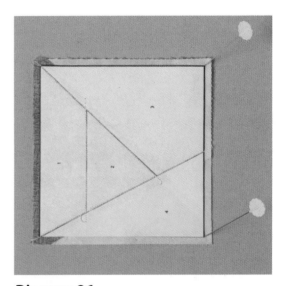

Diagram 26

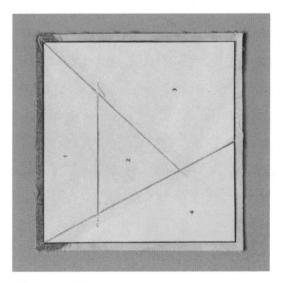

Diagram 27

Step 3: Press the sections open and continue sewing the sections in pairs. **(Diagram 28)**

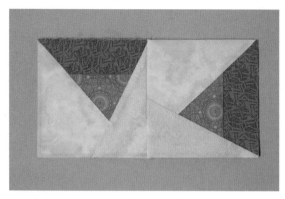

Diagram 28

Step 4: Sew necessary pairs of sections together to complete the block. **(Diagram 29)**

Diagram 29

The blocks are now ready to sew into your quilts.

What You Don't Want to Forget

1. If you plan to sew by hand, begin by taking some backstitches which will anchor the thread at the beginning of the line. Then use a backstitch every four or five stitches. End the stitching with a few backstitches.

2. If you plan to sew by machine, start stitching two or three stitches before the start of the stitching line and finish your stitching two or three stitches beyond the end.

3. Use a short stitch (about 20 stitches per inch) for paper foundations to make it easier to remove the paper. If the paper falls apart as you sew, your stitches are too short.

4. Finger press (or use an iron) each seam as you finish it.

5. Stitching which goes from a space into another space will not interfere with adding additional fabric pieces.

6. Remember to trim all seam allowances at least ¼".

7. When sewing points, start from the wide end and sew towards the point.

8. Unless you plan to use it only once in the block, it is a good idea to stay away from directional prints in foundation piecing.

9. When cutting pieces for foundation piecing, never worry about the grainline.

10. Always remember to sew on the marked side, placing the fabric on the unmarked side,

11. Follow the numerical order, or it won't work.

12. Once you have finished making a block, do not remove the paper until the entire quilt has been finished unless you stay stitch around the outside of the block.

13. Be sure that the ink you use to make your foundation is permanent and will not wash out into your fabric.

Making a Quilt

Sewing the Blocks Together

Once all of the blocks for your quilt have been made, place them on a flat surface such as a design wall or floor to decide on the best placement.

Sew the blocks together. You can do this by sewing the blocks in rows, then sewing the rows together; or, sew the blocks in pairs then sew pairs together. Continue sewing in pairs until entire quilt top is sewn together. **(Diagram 30)**

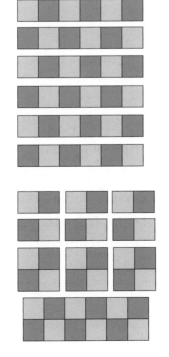

Diagram 30

Adding Borders

Borders are usually added to a quilt sides first, then top and bottom.

Simple Borders

Step 1: Measure the quilt top lengthwise and cut two border strips to that length by the width measurement given in the project instructions. Strips may have to be pieced to achieve the correct length. To make the joining seam less noticeable, sew the strips together diagonally. Place two strips right sides together at right angles. Sew a diagonal seam. **(Diagram 31)**

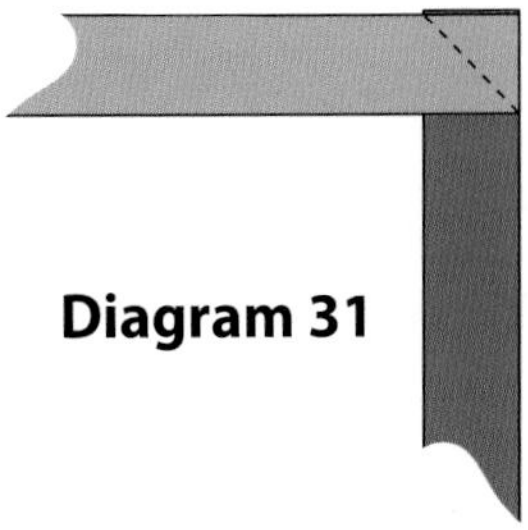

Diagram 31

Step 2: Trim excess fabric ¼" from stitching. **(Diagram 32)**

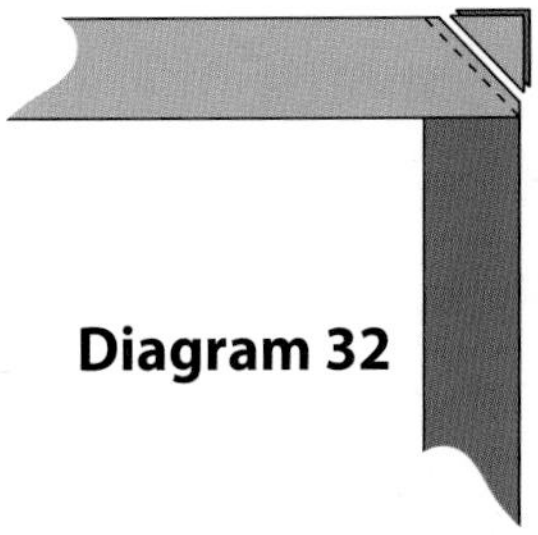

Diagram 32

Step 3: Press seam open. **(Diagram 33)**

Diagram 33

Step 4: Sew strips to the sides of the quilt. Now measure the quilt top crosswise, being sure to include the borders you have just added. Cut two border strips, following the width measurement given in the instructions.

Step 5: Add these borders to the top and bottom of the quilt. Repeat this process for any additional borders. Use the ¼" seam allowance at all times and press all of the seams to the darker side. Press the quilt top carefully.

Mitered Borders

Mitered borders are much more time-consuming, but sometimes the results may well be worth the effort.

Step 1: Measure the quilt top lengthwise. Cut two strips that length plus twice the finished border width plus ½" for seam allowances. Piece if necessary, referring to Step 1 in Simple Borders (Page 57).

Step 2: Measure the quilt top crosswise. Cut, piecing if necessary, two strips that length plus twice the finished border width plus ½".

Step 3: Find the midpoint of border strip by folding strip in half. **(Diagram 34)**

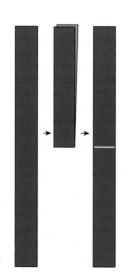

Diagram 34

Step 4: Place strip right sides together with quilt top matching midpoint of border with midpoint of quilt side. Pin in place. **(Diagram 35)**

Pin border to quilt top along entire side.

Step 5: Beginning ¼" from top edge, sew border strip to quilt top, ending ¼" from bottom edge. Backstitch at beginning and ending of sewing. **(Diagram 36)**

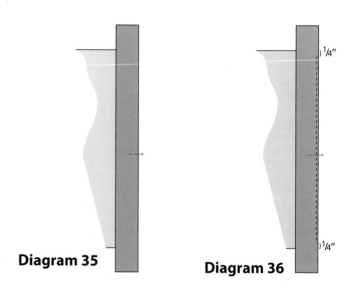

Diagram 35   Diagram 36

Step 6: To finish corners, fold quilt top in half diagonally right sides together; borders will extend straight up and away from quilt. Place ruler along folded edge of quilt top going into border strip; draw a diagonal line on the border. **(Diagram 37)**

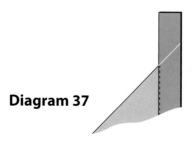

Diagram 37

58

Step 7: Beginning at corner of quilt top, stitch along drawn line to edge of border strip. **(Diagram 38)**

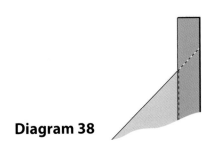

Diagram 38

Step 8: Open quilt at corner to check miter. If satisfied, trim excess fabric ¼" from diagonal seam. **(Diagram 39)**

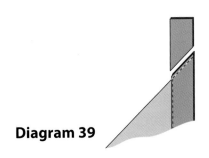

Diagram 39

Step 9: Repeat process on remaining three corners.

Finishing Your Quilt

Attaching the Batting and Backing

There are a number of different types of batting on the market today including the new fusible battings that eliminate the need for basting. Your choice of batting will depend upon how you are planning to use your quilt. If the quilt is to serve as a wall hanging, you will probably want to use a thin cotton batting. A quilt made with a thin cotton or cotton/polyester blend works best for machine quilting. Very thick polyester batting should be used only for tied quilts.

The best fabric for quilt backing is 100% cotton fabric. If your quilt is larger than the available fabric you will have to piece your backing fabric. When joining the fabric, try not to have a seam going down the center. Instead cut off the selvages and make a center strip that is about 36" wide and have narrower strips at the sides. Seam the pieces together and carefully iron the seams open. (This is one of the few times in making a quilt that a seam should be pressed open.) Several fabric manufacturers are now selling fabric in 90" or 108"-widths for use as backing fabric.

It is a good idea to remove the batting from its wrapping 24 hours before you plan to use it and open it out to full size. You will find that the batting will now lie flat when you are ready to use it.

The batting and the backing should be cut about one to two inches larger on all sides than the quilt top. Place the backing wrong side up on a flat surface. Smooth out the batting on top of this, matching the outer edges. Center the quilt top, right side up, on top of the batting.

Now the quilt layers must be held together before quilting, and there are several methods for doing this:

Safety-pin Basting: Starting from the center and working toward the edges, pin through all layers at one time with large safety pins. The pins should be placed no more than 4" apart. As you work, think of your quilting plan to make sure that the pins will avoid prospective quilting lines.

Thread Basting: Baste the three layers together with long stitches. Start in the center and sew toward the edges in a number of diagonal lines.

Quilt-gun Basting: This handy trigger tool pushes nylon tags through all layers of the quilt. Start in the center and work toward the outside edges. The tags should be placed about 4" apart. You can sew right over the tags, which can then be easily removed by cutting them off with scissors.

Spray or Heat-Set Basting: Several manufacturers have spray adhesives available especially for quilters. Apply these products by following the manufacturers' directions. You might want to test these products before you use them to make sure that they meet your requirements.

Fusible Iron-on Batting: These battings are a wonderful new way to hold quilt layers together without using any of the other time-consuming methods of basting. Again, you will want to test these battings to be certain that you are happy with the results. Follow the manufacturers' directions.

Quilting

If you like the process of hand quilting, you can–of course–finish these projects by hand quilting. However, if you want to finish these quilts quickly, in the time we are suggesting, you will want to use a sewing machine for quilting.

If you have never used a sewing machine for quilting, you may want to find a book and read about the technique. You do not need a special machine for quilting. Just make sure that your machine has been oiled and is in good working condition.

If you are going to do machine quilting, you should invest in an even-feed foot. This foot is designed to feed the top and bottom layers of a quilt evenly through the machine. The foot prevents puckers from forming as you machine quilt. Use a fine transparent nylon thread in the top and regular sewing thread in the bobbin.

Quilting in the ditch is one of the easiest ways to machine quilt.

This is a term used to describe stitching along the seam line between two pieces of fabric. Using your fingers, pull the blocks or pieces apart slightly and machine stitch right between the two pieces. The stitching will look better if you keep the stitching to the side of the seam that does not have the extra bulk of the seam allowance under it.

The quilting will be hidden in the seam.

Free-form machine quilting can be used to quilt around a design or to quilt a motif. The quilting is done with a darning foot and the feed dogs down on the sewing machine. It takes practice to master Free-form quilting because you are controlling the movement of the quilt under the needle rather than the sewing machine moving the quilt. You can quilt in any direction—up and down, side-to-side and even in circles—without pivoting the quilt around the needle. Practice this quilting method before trying it on your quilt.

Attaching the Continuous Machine Binding

Once the quilt has been quilted, it must be bound to cover the raw edges.

Step 1: Start by trimming the backing and batting even with the quilt top. Measure the quilt top and cut enough 2 ½" wide strips to go around all four sides of the quilt plus 12". Join the strips end to end with diagonal seams and trim the corners. **(Diagram 40)** Press the seams open.

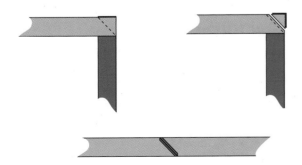

Diagram 40

Step 2: Cut one end of the strip at a 45-degree angle and press under ¼". **(Diagram 41)**

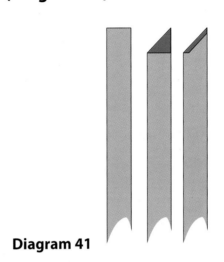

Diagram 41

Step 3: Press entire strip in half lengthwise, wrong sides together. **(Diagram 42)**

Step 4: On the back of the quilt, position the binding in the middle of one side, keeping the raw edges together. Sew the binding to the quilt with the ¼" seam allowance, beginning about three inches below the folded end of the binding. **(Diagram 43)**

Diagram 42

Diagram 43

At the corner, stop ¼" from the edge of the quilt and backstitch.

Step 5: Fold binding away from quilt so it is at a right angle to edge just sewn. Then, fold the binding back on itself so the fold is on the quilt edge and the raw edges are aligned with the adjacent side of the quilt. Begin sewing at the quilt edge. **(Diagram 44)**

Diagram 44

Step 6: Continue in the same way around the remaining sides of the quilt. Stop about 2" away from the starting point. Trim any excess binding and tuck it inside the folded end. Finish the stitching. **(Diagram 45)**

Diagram 45

Step 7: Fold the binding to the front of the quilt so the seam line is covered; machine-stitch the binding in place on the front of the quilt. Use a straight stitch or tiny zigzag with invisible or matching thread. If you have a sewing machine that does embroidery stitches, you may want to use your favorite stitch.

Adding a Rod Pocket

In order to hang your quilt for family and friends to enjoy, you will need to attach a rod pocket to the back.

Step 1: Cut a strip of fabric, 6" wide by the width of the quilt.

Step 2: Fold short ends of strip under ¼", then fold another ¼". Sew along first fold. **(Diagram 46)**

Diagram 46

Step 3: Fold strip lengthwise with wrong sides together. Sew along raw edges with a ¼" seam allowance to form a long tube. **(Diagram 47)**

Diagram 47

Step 4: Place tube on ironing surface with seam up and centered; press seam open and folds flat. **(Diagram 48)**

Diagram 48

Step 5: Place tube on back of quilt, seam side against quilt, about 1" from top edge and equal distance from side edges. **(Diagram 49)**

Diagram 49

Pin in place so tube is straight across quilt.

Step 6: Hand stitch top and bottom edges of tube to back of quilt being careful not to let stitches show on front of quilt.

Labeling Your Quilt

Always sign and date your quilt when finished. You can make a label by cross-stitching or embroidering or even writing on a label with a permanent marking pen on the back of your quilt. If you are friends with your computer, you can even create an attractive label on the computer.

Index